The Book of Awe

The Book of Awe

Poems

Susan O'Dell Underwood

Iris Press
Oak Ridge, Tennessee

Cover Photograph: "Fox"
Copyright © 2018 by David Underwood
www.underwoodartworks.com

Book Design: Robert B. Cumming, Jr.

Iris Press
www.irisbooks.com

Library of Congress Cataloging-in-Publication Data

Names: Underwood, Susan O'Dell, 1962- author.
Title: The book of awe : poems / Susan O'Dell Underwood.
Description: Oak Ridge, Tennessee : Iris Press, [2018]
Identifiers: LCCN 2018034815 | ISBN 9781604542486 (pbk. : alk. paper)
Classification: LCC PS3621.N388 A6 2018 | DDC 811/.6—dc23 LC record
available at https://lccn.loc.gov/2018034815

Acknowledgments

Grateful acknowledgment is made to the editors of the following publications, in which these poems first appeared, sometimes in earlier versions:

Alimentum: "Transubstantiation"
Blue Fifth Review Notebook: "Disciple"
EcoTheo Review: "Guilt"
Psaltery & Lyre: "Song," "Confession," and "Love"
Rock & Sling: "Worship," "Witness," "Magnificat," and "Hope"
Rockvale Review: "Prayer" and "Psalm"
Tusculum Review (website) for a special artist feature: "Gnosis" and "Annunciation"
Tusculum Review : "Poiesis"
TQ 14 (Tupelo Quarterly): "Theodicy"

Thank you to family, friends, colleagues, and dear students, without whom these poems could not have been written. Special thanks to Beto and Bob Cumming, and to Cathy Kodra for her expert editorial eye and love for poetry. And to all kinds of poet-friends and creative spirits whose insights and gumption inspire me. You know who you are!

for Dave, the awe of my life

Contents

Poiesis

Gnosis

APHESIS

EPILOGUE

POIESIS

Poiesis

In the beginning was the word.
John 1:1

In the dark so dark it glowers,
you wake,
not awake to thought, but sense
a word that shelters where the light can't reach,
a magnetic possibility in ocean canyons,
so far
it may well swim through galaxies.
It lumbers, tests its cool, safe skin,
resisting other skin
to know its perfect singularity,
beautifully, wonderfully monstrous,
turned over and over within its power,
untouched by power outside itself,
only the word coming to know its purity,
heaving up under the sweaty blankets
to touch mute distance closing fast
between the mind and the light,
seeking again the ken
between what is made and unmade,
made and unmade, diving and surfacing
back to the hapless repeated making and unmaking,
back to the strange eclipse
in which you recognize:
you are the field and also the page,
made so by the love which makes you,
which made you, turning on the axis of that breath
which breathes the very dust
alive with naming.

Firmament

The heavens and Heaven.
God and image.

Apples and oranges.
What's not to compare?
Each fruit an imperfect sphere,
tart and juicy with stem and seeds,
vulnerable to fall and rot, plunder of birds,
and worm-sting, the hunger of wasps.

An apple or an orange can settle right into the toe
of a little boy's Christmas stocking,
weight the bottom of his paper lunch sack,
roll around inside the picnic basket he'll remember
set open on the sand between his parents' toes
and the blue ocean's horizon.

Comparisons go on and on, eternal.
So why not bicycles and mountain goats?
Glaciers and peanuts? Rain and microscopes?
There will be snow falling around you
and the snow you walk in which has already fallen.

On the news you watch live footage of an astronaut
tethered to his space station, making repairs.
What could be more
opposite from human than space?
There's a fine slice of earth beyond him, finite,
and all you can think is,
That's such an awfully long way to fall.

How do you compare the long ago starlight
now visible and the stars to which
he's only a whisper closer than you?

You might imagine he is dangling like ripe fruit.
But this is nothing he considers, with his knowledge
of zero gravity and the absence of atmosphere.
He focuses on metal tools and protocol,
an apogee or perigee from sand dunes and cow beetles,
trout fishermen and hemlocks, whales
and crochet needles, hawks and earthquakes, so far
from apples and oranges
and the fat red pencils he loved as a boy
and the whole vivid ocean all at once now.

The earth lives turbulent but constant
in his periphery, without you visible
yet with you there all along, inconsequential
speck and soul.
Consequentially, you think
of running out into the yard
and looking up, to wave or to pray.

Dominion

What's the difference between the wildflower
and the name of the wildflower spoken aloud?
Each April you touch them and know their names:
lady slipper, blood root, trillium.
Hold each one's soft face close to your own.
They brush your lips if you say them right.
They color you with scent.

But the woods are vapor unless you also speak the woods
and speak, too, the trees lit high above with morning sky,
though where you stand is mossy dark with comfort
and the dripping finish of the night.

What Eve wanted—
more than she wanted flowers that woke when she woke,
their petal skin against her skin, the light and dark
separated for her—is what you yearn for still:
Speak them and they'll be known to you.

Forget there's good and evil if you want.

You can't forget the green leaves lisping along the limbs,
the meadow parsing breeze from hush,
and birds parleying in the trees.
You can't forget the buds
on the verge of wheedling bloom.
You can't forget the air she breathed in
just before she whispered
finally the word
and knew she was alive.

Sanctified

To yourself you are always an unquestionable given,
but there was a time before.
Does that terrify you like death to come?

To prove your long-ago long absence, pictures
of your parents—little children then themselves—
and all your people, gone, like others before you centuries gone,
and stars collapsed, and cosmic dust
dispersed and reassembled and dispersed.

There's a photograph of you in Utah
beneath the Delicate Arch—
that alpha parabola foot to foot, leg to leg.
Hewn out by driven sand, its queenly curvature
fairly hovers a thousand feet up on a sheer cliff ledge.
Any second, the shapely omega could fall and plummet,
could have fallen any second for a thousand, thousand years.

Then there are photographs of the arch alone.
But you did stand there.
You'll claim the day was hot
with only scrawny desert brush for shade.
You climbed with others up the slick rock steeps,
each your own way at your own pace.
You understood each other in strange languages.
You shared warm water and laughed.
Your muscles hurt. You breathed hard in and out.

At the top of the precipice, you crept beneath the arch
like a child on hands and knees.
Near the horrible edge you stretched your body out,
your head on red sandstone's warm
and perfect flesh, and looked up at the span

against the sky,
a barely balanced door.

You lay just moments until another traveler
wanted to see what you had seen, lie where you had been.
And no time later, walking away,
could it be as if you'd never been there,
unremembered by that place?

The arch straddled you,
the minutes it might take to eat an apple in the sun,
or undo the laces of your boots and slip them off,
a brevity that mundane and holy,
the time it takes to wash
fine red dust from your feet.

Revelation

In photographs of Manchester Beach, the Pacific
under fog fades beyond curling low brambles of pink.
Those blooming vines defy the bluster,
the gorgeous faith of roots against the sand's erosion.

Signs convince you, if everybody who wanted
to pick one bud gave in to temptation,
there'd be nothing left of the beach.
So home to Tennessee you carry only picture
after picture of exotic dunes,
like graves of kites festooned with tufting flowers.

Your father looks at the first photo and declares, "Vetch,"
a weed as common as mullein or Queen Anne's lace,
more plentiful than chicory or Joe-Pye weed,
tedious as Johnson grass and that blasted multi-flora rose.

How did you not recognize *vetch*,
all around you your whole life,
never once an urge to know?

Every June to come, after redbuds and laurel
and dogwoods go dingy,
you watch for vetch, its faint chaos
remarking every ditch and fence row,
stubborn shy in kudzu shade.

Vetch ranges its pale crawling mark,
a foundling whisper in the green chorus,
abundant and lowly, a brambling itch of a syllable
to pin down prophecy and whimsy too.

It'll keep teaching you:
there is no place so small it doesn't need a name.

Church

A long time ago, two or more of you gathered
in a field and wove white clover chains
to adorn your wrists and necks,
effortless halos round each head.

Day-long you plucked tender stems without one thought
of time or reward, or even dinner waiting on the table.
In that pasture
no sermon or the hubris of public prayer,
no responsive reading or hymn,
no calendar for baptism into belonging,
no conscripted Christian soldiers.

Into that sanctuary you came and went as you pleased
to braid the commonest beauty to yourselves
and carried home the spice of lowly grasses,
snowy wads of weed that wilted in the sun against your sweat.
No one admonished one another
to grieve or speak of sacrifice.
No weeping gratitude for what you believed
would come again into a thousand tomorrows,
without brick or mortar or the passing plate
or ritual hats and gloves and suits and ties.
No one coveted anyone else's ringlet
of humble blooms or worshiping voice.
Your singing twined together one anonymous song
beneath the infinite cool-domed blue.

There will never be again an ear
more willing than that wild, wild field.

Faith

for Wade Bibb

Look over your shoulder and take a deep breath.
Forget your new shoes that pinch,
the expensive cut of cloth you wear now,
the pristine gloss of your well-arranged life.
Back there everything is worn flannel and wool,
dust in the barn's soft dark,
the sound of your grandfather's coveralls whisking
as he lifts pitchfork after pitchfork of clean straw
into the stall you've just mucked out.
From this distance the work doesn't seem hard.
Did it ever seem like work when you were a child?
There was never one star-prick of doubt
that he made everything happen—the mule to move,
though its haunches wanted rest,
the plow edge to drive its beveled lines,
the corn in the pasture-field to tassel.
At the bare whim of his shoveling,
the creek diverted its stubborn course.
He decided when work was done, time to rest.
Come back to the house, over full plates
of potatoes and beans and squash he'd grown,
he would bow his head and speak in thanksgiving
as if he hadn't lifted a finger
and it had all been given to him.
Late, he made kindling he had cut
catch against impossible dampness.
In that heat the smell would rise up of soil and sweat.
You carry that smell, you hear?
You carry it and don't forget—his smell
as he taught you the work, and the warm musk
of the mule's hard-worked worthy hide and muscle.
Remember, you had to reach tall, stretching on tiptoe

to sweep the soft brush across the mule's broad back,
in careful devotion for the way he showed you
how it ought to be done.

Prayer

Stand at the canyon at sunrise
to watch the last dark become shadow,
to watch the shadows of morning drain like water.
The walls fill downward with light
you would never have believed before now.
Faith would never, not for an eternity, have been enough.
You have to witness for yourself.
The birdsong lifts the sky into being,
beaks and tongues and heat blooming into day,
as if the sun comes out of the ruby nests of their throats,
as if they sing the scent of juniper and pinyon,
as if they sing you, here.
You should believe enough now
to throw yourself from the rim.
Walk to the edge, as if you could walk
across the praise of day, as if you could fly.
But it is enough to practice throwing your voice
like a naked body, the one you were born into,
off the red lip of the canyon.
It is enough to whisper,
until you learn well enough
that there is nothing you need to say.

Witness

Once in a restive bookstore, across a shelf:
rustling grunts and plosive whispers,
loud pages whisking back and forth.
Down that aisle of books, a group of girls
in uniforms from the school for deaf children
signed to each other one-handed, tipsy-handed,
balancing birthing books and sex guides,
all grimacing with moans and giggling slaps
in spasms of disbelief
over the garish startle of blood and ecstasy.

Only librarians and mothers might wish for
a golden nothing, a molten rich beguiling absence.
Silence is not the mythic stone zero of the deaf.
There is always at least a pale roar,
an incessant conch whispering in the core of the brain.

Go to the mountains where not even a plane
passes overhead, not a motorized moment for aeons.
You come back and try hard as you can to prove
how silence really sounds, the trickle and creep,
the echo of underground pudge turning upward,
leaves sighing at the ends of their stems.
Try and describe the crawling scamper
twisting sideways through your ears,
a tickle and a pouting whimper,
the restlessness of the whole being world
with you moving in it.

Listen, you can't say what you can't say:
the fox, there, come down to the edge of the woods.

Worship

To keep the bear at bay
you sing while you go walking,
walking on the word of God,
breathing Allah in one long breath,
taking all the time in the world that Buddha will allow.

Call out your presence
through the thickest sapling groves and laurel hells,
trampling through the hedges and the fencerows.
Seek any song that saves you
from living life in fear of the bear,
or because of the bear, or avoiding the bear,
leery and distracted from the wonder.

Enough you'll know sometime, somewhere
the wild inevitable beauty,
strangely awful-seeming only here and now.
You'll understand it by and by somehow—
the necessary, regal beating heart
beneath the fur, the fur as deep as life itself,
the teeth like sharp moons,
incisors big as claws, the claws
around your bleeding, cradled head.

Psalm

That which makes you lie down in green clover,
urge light as breath against your breastbone.

Or the green itself will pull you down
into shade pooling like a body of water.

A tangling will ribbon its way to your knees
till supplicant then prostrate you give way,
an echo of the child again
pressed to the planet's pulse the way you lay
before you ever knew a prayer by heart
but only hummed a version
of the humming all around you.

Listen where you loll, and be.
That's praise you feel, that surge of comfort
where your head rests in the plush,
your thrumming feet and body languid in repose
while all around you dances, nothing ever still,
the scent of tender green in praise of you
for knowing how to notice, for minding
with your fingertips the rounded, fragile petals.

The craving soil itself is rapt with quivering,
filled up with that which makes you lie down among,
lie down within, against, toward,
that rousing quiet held which holds you here,
the shape your body makes, the remedy and jolt,
the ways to answer that which made you
to lie down in your whole singing flesh.

That which made you
made you to lie down in green clover.

Sermon

How many pencils do you think a Sequoia tree would make?
The park ranger asks the campfire crowd.
First-generation children breathe translations
to their mothers and fathers in Spanish.
There is no correct answer in any language.
Can you believe this was
the use manifest destiny dreamed up
for creation's heaviest trees? An abundance
of yellow #2s bundled in every desk cup?

Who was it—white, educated, moneyed—with hubris
to believe he discovered these giants? He ordered
the largest specimen peeled, left standing to rot without bark,
because civilization would never believe such a tree
without proof, taking nothing on faith.
No machine could carry the whole mass of flesh,
so rail cars transported only the tree's outer skin,
slashed off in patches, then quilted back together,
a sacrificial, freakish shroud displayed in city after city.

Which miracle doesn't begin with necessity
and a question? There is always human intercession,
or else only nature blooming its ineffable self
into the universe, unremarked, unremarkable.
The Sequoia cone, marvel how it measures in relation
to a child's upturned fist, just about to open
and release its seed, tiny as a flake of oatmeal,
falling its slow descent two hundred feet,
a weightless nourishment for the mystery.

What saved the Sequoias was snow and hunger.
And farmers, the ranger preaches. Logged mountainsides
would have eroded in muddy, avalanching waste.
Farmers knew the trees would magnify the sweet, white

deep of winter, frozen on every needle, cone, and limb.
This is the harvest gospel carried every spring
down from the Sierras: miraculous snowfalls
running to snowmelt creeks and rivers,
flowing from the mount to the San Joaquin Valley.

Where the groves begin and end, you can't see,
lost in the Valley's gridded farmland. You drive
on faith and narrow lanes between miles of avocado
and artichoke fields, through vast orchards
green and alive without human movement, a rapture of food.
Finally you find men on ladders, picking apples.
None of them speaks English. "El Patron—"
They point to the foreman. Servants
of the richest soil provide the way with their hands.

When you're gone, they will climb into trees and walk field rows
all day, all week, all month, all summer.
They'll feed multitudes with asparagus, berries, broccoli,
cauliflower, nectarines, peaches, peppers, spinach, zucchini,
a bounty they name with words you never learn.
But the miracle translation is from flesh to flesh.
Whenever you eat an orange, the ranger told you, *stop.*
Think for just a moment of the water that grew it,
water which was snow once, held on winter limbs.

Did you know he was teaching you how to pray?

Disciple

You eat Utah,
literal salt of the earth,
briny efflorescence of an ancient shoreline.
Eat the rust-iron pink and shimmer-silver,
the turquoise and sulfur-yellow encrusting
the ruptured bedrock
you walked across in summer sun.

Your sweat as it rose up to evaporate
tasted on your lip
exactly like that vast millennial sea.

Deep in winter's early dark,
you crave that brackish life,
no slap-dash dash and sprinkle,
but appetites immersed in tart salinity.
Salt infuses every form—the gumbo's roux,
the simplest of Sunday eggs,
homemade oatmeal cookies' savory sass.
Nothing pure or cautious here in this house.
You cook by finger and touch, tonguing
and eyeing and hefting.

You would sift your very self down into buttery grease,
into the rise and mellow swell of dough,
the way you gave yourself up to the wilderness,
wishing you could enter Zion's desert rock,
your raw, redeemed life
boiled down to dry blood, erupted
minerals stunned in the blue-hard sunlight.

GNOSIS

Gnosis

When the bird and the book disagree, believe the bird.
—John James Audubon

I can't give you everything I know,
even if I wished nature held that kind of sway.
Take for example the thousand heads
I want to show you of grasshopper weeds,
their tips like fragile, flaming fleece,
bobbing one wave in the final pentecost of dusk.

Go with me while I walk,
each step forward a step back.
Think to the days our grandmothers lived,
younger than we are now, when they staved
off long as they could their smallest fears of thunderstorms,
and the worst—their children coming to early harm.
Such deaths might not have happened
right in front of them, but did.

The train passes with its blast just when we've crossed.
We wait out time and boxcars, recross the tracks,
retrace our steps, though we can never
really be the same place over
or live another's life, or know another being's joy or fears.
Yet can't we feel the seismic passages, as if they're ours?

Look and listen. I will give you everything I can,
you give me yours, this moment, when twilight spans
the purpling sky, such sudden dark
above us that we're taken aback
by clumsy blindness,
blind to even one winging shadow of the geese,
so close we hear their plumage work. They honk invisible.
But hold on to your faith, ridiculous, insensible.

They must be there if you can hear them.
They must be there, even if you can't see them.
What's there is there. *What's there?*
Nothing ever stays in place for long, like a rare
and fleeting evening star. You blink,
it's gone. No need to bow in praise or thanks.

The world won't
run because of what you pray or don't.
It runs despite us,
driven as the faithful geese
who rant their V into the tired night, long miles away,
where someone else looks up now, trying to see them go.

Judgment

Witness
the hellish life of the neighbor lady's terrier, blind
with eyes like moonstone pools of milk,
so deaf it can't hear,
not even when you hold it up—
its scrawny, trembling ribcage in one hand—
and whistle right into its ear.
It would take only your fist
clenched tight around its neck,
a torquing jolt to end the misery.
Whose misery?
You've asked your neighbor to her face
to end its pain. But she'd be lost, she says,
inside her empty, lonely house.
She loves her nasty little creature like a darling.
Nearly toothless, greasy as a rat,
the dog goes spiraling its waddling search
for a place to piss and shit
in tall grass to its nose.
It hunches its hind quarters,
strains and aims again,
bumping its face against a stone,
an ivied wall, reversing like a clumsy toy,
circling in silent darkness for relief,
its tiny world made more immense
because it knows less day by day.
You know more
because you learn to see and suffer
all its suffering.

Pity

Jesus neglected to mention
that one of the least of these
might hold a knife to your throat.

Even this weary old woman
walking along the highway
alone on the coldest day of the year, bent
by bags of groceries tugging
at her bare hands.

A widow or a lunatic will walk the same,
pathetic without coat or hat,
dressed in winter as if for April,
crucifixion weather.

Good intentions and good sense
wrestle like Jacob in you.
There's the matter of sanity, then dignity.
Even if she's got her wherewithal,
she might just pitch a hissy fit
against your no-good do-good meddling,
your hand-me-down hand-out.
She's not some charity case
or a star for your crown.

So as not to offend,
you sin again the sin most sinned
of risking nothing.
The day will move the way
it would have moved all along.

But she will follow you home,
this stray who goads you to begrudge
the lesson, the bullying plague of doing unto,
which you have left again undone.

Charity

Mold on this bread is as natural as the morning sun
that steams up your kitchen in the first place.
Yet you feel ashamed, standing in the light
to rout out the cloud-blue blight
and sniff each crust for blemishes you can't see.
What you can salvage you pinch and pinch,
a massacre of holes a finger would fit,
only fit for toast you'll eat yourself.
The worst you'll grind into crumbs for birds.

Imagine the ones who might judge you
as you hold up one piece of bread
after another to your face,
and put the plucked remainder back in the bag.
They would not think communion
or hunger but only:
Oh. That's how these people are.

It's easy to deride yourself
for managing such a poverty of bread.
Salve your self-doubt. Remember
the recent Sunday dinner your father pushed back
from his clean plate, as if he realized just then
how poor his childhood was, as if he prayed:
"The little girl on the farm next to us starved to death one winter."
This is a memory your mother says
he has never, in fifty years, said out loud to her.

Now there's no one here to judge you but yourself,
eating what you could handily throw away,
throwing away what you ought to have eaten,
caught between domestic crimes,
believing your life depends upon this choice
because somewhere someone else's always will.

Communion

for Krista Reese

Alone and cooking in your kitchen,
throw a party larger than the party you have planned.

Carrots keep you company by the pound.
You muscle them, scrubbed clean as cooks have scrubbed
since carrots ever were, then chop them lively
with the handsome knife your cousin bought you.
Think about him far away while
all the while you pile up onions and potatoes
in your great aunts' footed colander,
the old one, galvanized, with holes arranged like stars.
Set out the crackled china platter
your grandmother used for half a century.

Let the unknown keep you company too—
vintner, dairyman, orchard keeper,
the one who risked his life to catch this fish,
the someone else who spends her day-long life
cradling brown eggs into cartons.
Think while you string and break green beans
of those who stoop all day through rows.

Who harvests the olives and presses the oil?
Who else begins each day
with blood and slaughter, cures
and slices miracle-thin prosciutto?
Who hauls the melons from the fields?
Then sifting flour, picture those who thresh the wheat,
who pluck the berries for your pie,
who turn cane into sugar for the perfect rind
you'll blaze onto the crème brûlée.

And farther back, you think of those who long ago begat,
the ones who figured out the way to salvage rot,
discovered clabbered milk by chance, and moldy cheese,
and raisins shriveled in the heat, who praised
the mother of all vinegar, the hapless start of soured dough,
whose faith brined the toughest chicken in the pot to succulence.

By the time the timer rings, you've welcomed in a holy host—
old friends alive in recipes they wrote by hand
on grease-marked little cards
or on the backs of envelopes gone dark.
You bring their fellowship to light,
the nexus of the spice route where you stand
right now with tarragon in hand, with rosemary
and lavender and coriander. You transform
the bitter, salt and sweet, the sour,
the piquant savory born again into *umami*.

Your final offering the body of stout, hearty bread,
the flagrant wine's finesse.

Your palate shapes most pleased
around the simplest phrase you love to say to those you love:
"Dinner's ready. Come sit down and eat. Everybody."

Blessing

You talk aloud to the rare bones and meat
on your plate, quoting Blake:
*"Little Lamb who made thee,
Dost thou know who made thee."*

No question marks the poet's version.
And you aren't asking either.
It is done.
Heavy with impossible answers,
you slide the knife blade into flesh.
The only rhetoric is violence.
This sacrifice will nourish you,
as you know
you are meant to nourish
everything around you in return.

A little guilt goes down like salt,
inside a prayer or out,
a meager nod to blood and gore
acknowledging that you are likewise
only passing through.
One tender bite, you taste the suffering to come,
staved off once more like hunger
in an amnesty of crystal candlelight,
the luxurious tablecloth white as wool.

Your instinct is to bleat.

Annunciation

You have to believe this gospel is man-made,
the oil paint luminous as pain,
the angel dressed in blood red.

No woman would frame this sacred moment
inside a gilded trap so garish and so public.
No woman gestates willfully
the glory of certain death.
Here is sacrifice forced upon her,
the rapturous horn-blast
boggling the brainstem into panic,
a consecration, a conscription.

Against your will you must imagine
the mother who can't stop imagining the tank,
against all odds blown over on its side,
the undercarriage a cavity,
the manufactured shell of steel
a caved-in womb, a tomb.

It's a man of glory who comes knocking
to inform each mother too late
about the end of time
she carried once
inside her body like a bomb.

Magnificat

How the forest magnifies your soul,
the way the forest is magnified by the creek,
and the creek magnified by ten thousand fevered salmon.
Mothers-to-be, each and every handmaiden
gives herself, willful
with the greater will that pushes forward
into the muscling water.

This is the violence of maternity, without mercy.
Whether you stand amazed or not,
whether you believe this marvel blesses you,
each silver servant swims her doomed and blessed path.
They bite one another in gaping, vicious mouthfuls
down to pink flesh, down to spine and bone,
thrashing the water to a blind, boiling panic
with their wounded, bloody blurs,
a frenzied, warring cannibal cabal
racing for the perfect place to lay down creation,
then lay their brief lives down.

Bodies drift, dead-eyed graying sacrificial piles
caught along the bank among deadfall debris.
Still the living swim,
spiking tail against stone to climb over the weak,
stumbling over each other, over the dead,
moving forever and ever, it seems, up the writhing stream,
each lowliest of the lowly waging her prophecy.

Transubstantiation

Even if this rainbow trout were still alive,
there would be no way to know
how many days or what kinds of skies
it saw or understood
before that jaw-twisting pierce and jerk
slung it upward into mid-air, or even then
whether it perceived the plainest blue light as above
or below, and itself as reaching or falling or flying
in the first moment of its dying,
but its silver skin seems alive even now,
streaked with indigo blue-grey, pink, and green
under the plunging last cleanse of ice water,
staring its dead-eye dare up from the stainless bowl
as if it might yet find a rock to winnow around,
searching for the familiar brown serenity of stones
and the pleasure of colorless shadow,
its body the shiniest blaze
that could ever have mattered
in the sleek, narrow, steadfast world it lived within;
even now it means more than the namesake
praising its resemblance,
more than this prism of a word.

Hubris

140-Year-Old Lobster Freed—
Restaurant Liberates Lobster Centenarian

Everyone who reads the headline wonders:
Where will he go?
He's scarred, fighting for survival
every day since the War Between the States,
reigning his kingdom's cold black depths
longer than any human ever lived.
Lucky curmudgeon. You imagine
his huge red claws like bulbous parentheses
around our measly history.

Maybe he was ready to be done with it, though.
He let himself drift with the currents
right into the trap, hefted up with common others
clattering and dripping in one haul onto the deck,
his last act of free will a democratic gesture.

But he didn't foresee the emasculating rubber bands,
the impoverished corners of the tank,
the water roiling rank with stupid adolescent lobsters
who jar and jockey over nothing.
Entitled brats, unaware of the prowess of his youth,
longevity they'll never reach.
And ignorant of their imminent deaths,
snatched up one by one by the random,
reaching mongers from above.

This abject surrender wasn't in his plan.
How undignified to depend on higher powers
who grant random empathy only to the heroic
or infirm, the bizarre lesser than.

He relied, like a fool,
on the beneficent whim of unsteady creatures
whose appetites will run always to the self,
those who can't decree reprieve for a tough old lobster
without publishing their deed.

So here's your glory in the media,
how nobly once you ceded your dominion.
Huzzah! You freed the ancient lobster
from being boiled alive, salvation
from the rapturous devouring.

Then, too, poems will be written to further explain.

You forget: *Only the lobster knows the real story.*

Song

At five in the morning,
the lightest touch of arm against arm,
a sleepy gesture so tender—hand silk-hair rubbing,
the clumsy buss of lips against forehead—
then the eyes open, tongues
find their breathy praise in the dark,
every cell aching toward another,
and you live again in skin and sweat,
as if you're twenty-two and new at this
and not a quarter-century married.

Live up to the upstart ruckus
you show your students every spring.
As you usher wayward bees out the classroom window,
you point toward the pollinated green
and wait for their embarrassed giggles:
"See? Look. Everything is having sex."

The two of you bask with the covers thrown back,
catch your breath in the dawn's warm April air
through your open bedroom window.
Congratulate yourselves you've made a vow
with more than one another.
You've joined the wonderful want that never stops.
Why worry that the neighbors might have heard you
doing your part to make the planet turn?

Dare the wish you dare to wish on morning's last star:
that every creature be mated and warm,
every couple coupled and quickened,
married fresh in the sweet, dark dawn,
each one known and knowing.

You can't for one pulse of your blood believe
the two of you alone
have woken every singing bird in the county.

Temptation

Nothing but a pretty notion at first,
harmless as the fish that glide behind glass walls,
rubbing one another raw
and never getting anywhere.
In your idle mind you mull the bright and nimble toy,
the lure, the spinning jig you want to be.

In the aquarium, otters and the bovine manatees,
the hammerhead sharks and clownfish,
even the Beluga whales fin in only vague distractions.
You want to fascinate, electrify, to undulate
like gorgeous jellyfish, with power
that projects the ache to touch and be touched.

You'll flicker a medusa of bioluminescent tangles,
ignore the vast dimension of every danger.
Put on your ploy of fluttering light,
the wavering gentle tendrils of illusion.

This coy deception meant to fool
can only fool your self the most.
No one's immune to this bright, bubbling anguish.
No one walks forever blithely past
such narrowly restrained high walls of water,
a yearning like the sea divided.

These pretty colors and their shapes withheld,
unreachable, belie a tapestry of water
in which you'd surely drown,
trapped and struggling against the want
of your own want,
the lash and sting, the ugly welt
of you reflected in the glass.

Jealousy

How can bodies move like that in sunlight,
oblivious as palomino ponies, nearly floating,
fetlock, flank, and hoof impervious to rocky ground?
Everything for them is always wave after
effortless wave of grand breath,
never knowing what it means
to have to think to breathe.

And you, stuck in a barrel,
salted flesh aware of every nerve and pore,
each tinge a misery, too hot, too cold,
too wet, too thirsty,
hungry, naked.

The brutal hug of wanting more
is all you feel,
where your skin stops and the air starts.
That keening cry you carry hurts,
incessant whimpering your mission
without the time or light or will to notice
how your blue toenails and gray lips
long ago went pink with life,
a bounty outside your regard.

Hold on there to the dark,
the smothered burden smothering.
Nurse your lead-heavy pang,
an easy worship fit for every unsung king.
Crown yourself.
Listen way down there forever
to the echo of what you can't have.

Spite

You thwart your own peace.
Steer yourself into this swamp,
devoured and drowning in its flesh.

Come on in, the cancer is warm;
the black waters will buoy you.

Only the first step takes you any nerve at all,
the squish of what once lived and breathed
now rotten in between your toes,
the muck of some other self that's halved itself
and halved those suicidal selves to bones and skin
until the particles putrefy.

See the queenly cypress die
by the slow-hand choke of strangler figs.
Malignant ropes of vine crawl tightening
their brazen brawn to lattice the last collapse
of brittle bark until they kill themselves
with the hurt they aim to do.

This putrid silt will moor you,
slick and sucking under.
Given every chance to go, you grovel
in the slime, and gorge on every seething grudge.

You are your own reptilian brain's last meal,
your own slit-eyed winking monster.
Primordial thrash and drag of ugly tow
will twist the rank gut-spill of you.
Mired down in fetid green,
you'll lose yourself, fingernail, tongue,
scalp, and eyeball, digested inside out.

Exile

Six-Mile Cypress Slough closes at sunset.
The tannic water seethes at dusk
as if fine rain were falling.
The swamp's black-mirror surface bubbles,
brewing its minutiae of insect millions
straining for survival.

What they thrive on is invisible.
What would eat them is edible.
What would eat you might be out there
in the fading light you hurry through.

Watch for black bears foraging, and panthers,
though they're mostly seen dead along the highways.
Alligators clock your twilight walk
with bellowed croaks, vying
with the nearby airstrip's droning buzz.
Snowy egrets and white herons roost their heavy glow
in trees that flank the roaring interstate.
Shopping plazas and pavement eat the swamp.

Then know, the giant here is you,
clomping along the darkening boardwalk
untouched by strangling vines and toothy palmettos,
holding handrails that mark safe boundary
between what's human and what isn't.

People call the cypress roots "knees,"
a presumptuous name.
To you they look like fingers.
But that's the same personifying ploy again.
You're arrogant to think
the new-born flesh of cypress points at you
with recrimination, rising up out of the murk,
drowned to the knucklebone.

Apocalypse

A tree is not a sentient being,
you tell yourself with each step deeper
into the old growth hemlock grove.

They reach above into the blue back-lit anonymous
to which you once looked in presumptuous prayer.
You're too late, arrogant
to think your voice could save the hoary limbs.
This blight is the craven end
and nothing of the revelation you used to believe.

Vigilant in all the wrong directions,
you waited for the prophesied nobility of fire,
the scathing beast that lunges,
practiced in the algorithm for rapture and ascent.

There never was forever-after waiting up above.

A tree is not a sentient being,
you pray now to believe.
Bedraggled elders droop their crowns
in acid keening silence.
Their broad girth lingers,
murdered in the deep wood's shade.

Ten winters more and here will be
deadfall collapse, a heap of grief where giants stood,
a rotten accusation, and you knee-deep
in the ruined forest of our making.

A tree is not a sentient being.
And yet you're watched and judged here.
You stand condemned, in horror of your naked
reckoning: *this*—this wood, this world—
was Eden, wasted on us all.

Hell

One spring the birds came up from bayou bays
and farther south, from jungle canopies
and splendid forest swamps,
to find themselves cast out.
Tired of flying in formation, instinct
in them yearning for the place they'd settled down
along their way for centuries before—
in the marshy cool of Turkey Creek
before a human granted it a name,
or winging for one migratory night
to hardwoods high on ancient mountainsides—
they found that in the year they'd been away
you paved their sanctuaries over,
tore down the curving pinnacle horizon.
No place to land.
Decapitated mountaintops
like fetid mesas ranged into forever,
coal-sludge dumped into caustic streams below.
Rewrite your version of the verse upon the land,
your faith in only what your power does,
your sole reward to benefit yourself,
your greedy pulse that drains the wetlands,
fractures earth, and slays square miles of trees
until there's nothing left
of God himself to stop you.
You can't grow wings to fly yourself away,
and so you never thought to watch the birds
or the paradise they tried to show you,
circling in their weary search above
until the very end when they fell dead
in massive plagues of feathered bodies,
thundering their murdered hailstorm
black as coal down from the sky, erased
for all eternity, but luckier than you
who never once looked up.

Theodicy

It's a small world, but not if you have to clean it.
—Barbara Kruger

Out in the ruined Gulf of Mexico, a live feed
records the worst we can do to ourselves.

No plague of biblical proportion ever came close to this mess.

Watch the visage of the violence—
the damaged brown pelicans,
black-slick hermit crabs and sand pipers,
mangrove roots and saw grass smothering in oil.
You take in vain again the names—*God* and *Good Lord*,
and the desperate worst-of-all, *Jesus Christ*.
There's no evidence any omnipotent being
so much as eavesdrops.

Like oil and water, your mother used to say
about your brother and you, exempting herself
like a wise Old Testament king,
backing out of the catastrophe.

You can't remember which of you drew first blood,
crying over tooth marks on your knuckles.
Who saw and thought your brother
sank his baby teeth into your hand?
Who saw and thought instead
that you had bashed him in the mouth?

In every Cain and Abel death-match of blame,
only impotence is unimpeachable.
Keep yourself out of the fray.

There's nothing left to hold against the love
that used to turn a different world
or justify the rage that can't leave
well enough alone in all this dark.
You can't do a thing to staunch
the Gulf's floor bloodletting
a mile down in freezing, pressurized black,
the most urgent voice the planet can muster.

Let the saviors be. One foolish human at a time
will wash one gull at a time, one heron,
cradle and redeem some big-winged creature.

Every last one is sent back to be sullied all over again.
Every last one of us stranded
like white bears in a faraway, melting land,
blinded like sheep on the steppes of Patagonia,
toxic and damaged, corrupted like spring peepers
waddling forward bright-eyed, on five legs.

Death

In the daybreak dream so real it feels like memory,
you watch from your squat hut's open window
as far gray gases boil their thunderhead,
and pyroclastic clouds of ash
blast cascades down the mountain.

Screams tear from the sloping fields,
and shouts of runners pass your doorway,
bare feet slapping down the dirt path,
sounds that even in your dream you know have been
the last sounds made at Krakatoa and Pompeii.

A shade consumes the muffled room you're standing in,
as if a harmless cumulus crossed the valley.
So real the dream:
the first touch on your skin and in your mouth
is steam, and then the subterranean sulfur fills your nostrils.

How quick it's done, your mind thinks in the dream.

When clots of stone as big as heads
crash down with darkness on your roof,
you know this plague that killed before will kill you too.
You reason there's no reason,
yet you turn and flee with all the rest,
out and over the walls around your house
and up and up the darkening hills
until the steepness overtakes you.
You dread your lungs seared with ash,
and while you sleep you hold your breath,
and when you wake and gasp in air,
your first thought is
that you alone survived, though you know
nothing saves you
from the native ruin coming to us all.

APHESIS

Aphesis

The magistrate sits in your heart that judges you.
—Elizabeth Proctor, Arthur Miller's *The Crucible*

The soul is nowhere you could name inside or out,
a phantom swoop at best, nocturnal flutter lost to light,
a weight of superstitious nothing.

The heart, though, beats and hurts, an aching place,
a warring thud against your ribs,
as if a hammer to the moral thumb, or sometimes
sharp and shocking as the papercut of conscience.

What river mouth can you find deep enough
to wash you back to your clean, nascent pulse?

Go—to what is now a filthy shore—alone.
Your veins and arteries are clogged
like deltas fanned with sand.
The stench of every burden washed up there
astounds your sense, the cull and trash you thought
you'd left behind, the rot of wasted days,
the swill of hateful perfidy and inside jokes
that leach your goodness, ugly words you can't digest,
the pox you wished on everyone.

Wade or dive or sink.
Tilt back your head and hold your breath,
baptized into the rhythm of your sins,
the stay-put push and tug that courses round
and round and carries you back toward yourself.

You'll find a riptide you can barely tread.
Grapple and submit each day to live
a rescued yet an always drowning life,
buoyed by the dark, persistent muscle you redeem.

Guilt

The ones who died? You magnify them
with your living, don't you?
On a Wednesday morning, think how good
they would think they had it, even when
it's raining again and making coffee is a chore
and leftover laundry has gone dank and spoiled,
deviling the corner with the sweat of your lost work.

The people you fix yourself to meet
are not yet ghosts, or otherwise
you'd put more stock in them, and sympathy,
and mercy too.

Instead they're heavy on you like the air before a storm,
or the elbow of a difficult triangle leaning forever.
They are sand and gravel in your pockets
as you approach the river's edge.

You can't say to them—can you?—*You're
the worst part of my day.*

Count ten, pretend
to have a better vantage from the ceiling,
from the treetop just outside the window,
or farther—from the eye of that tilting buzzard
in front of that smudge of ugly cloud.

There's nothing aerial in God's judgment.
So be the mote for just a moment.
Think mote-like while you're floating
tangled at the back of your own eye.
There's more trespass than you'll be able to amend.
You'll be too late beyond the grave,

gritting your rotted jaw, clenched forever
against what good you might have said,
instead of what you said.

Prophecy

for Tsuruoka Harumi, after the 2011 tsunami

Forsythia blooms
speak their yellow in the rain
like a burning bush.

Imagine if the slightest touch
of their cold voices could singe your skin.

It's dark now in Japan,
where fallout for the moment
is only snow.
This is the Ides of March, days after ruptured depths
roused houses into fiery tongues and ash,
where the ocean broke the shoreline's promise.

It's easy to blame the dead.

How did they not hear bird call stop,
follow all the brush creatures
skittering up into the hillsides?
Who among them could not feel the slight shift
of the planet's axis in their lungs, and run?
A tidal wave is foreseen, foretold.
It will happen again, the core broken open
eventually for every one of us.

Right now, old men and women pick up bricks
as if the bodies of children.
Families camp like refugees.
In hazmat suits, men throw themselves
into the manmade magma
of radioactive isotopes, as if their sacrifice
might un-divide the voice, throw back
the spark that started the whole universe.

They know their every death
is at the hands of fire, invisible, free-floating in the air,
a second-sight, the way you sometimes crave
to go ahead and face the worst that doom can do,
calamity you know you won't escape.

Curiosity will seize you like a stork's beak.
You see there in their plague all future chaos
made miniature, like the oracle in ancient golden scrolls:
Amid the brushstroke flurry of kimonos,
the grimace at the nucleus,
a delicate hand forever outstretched, reaching
for the last hand plunging
toward deliverance from a desecrated sea.

Hope

Climb up the dust, the stony trail,
to the place called "Weeping Rock,"
and stand inside its craggy amphitheater
hundreds of feet up the canyon wall,
fit for a Shakespearean portico
where lovers cry, staged
behind its constant curtain of mourning waters.

Theatrics here are geologically ponderous,
not human, as the name suggests.
The temptation was here long before you came
to personify the drama playing out eternally,
the overhanging ledge that seems to weep,
stone as red as the torn-open heart's flesh,
and fragile columbine in clusters
high on the canyon wall, so in love with heights.

You'd rather think the name intends
the place is overwhelmed for joy,
the leaping splash a bliss of transport.
Rare desert rain seeps a thousand years or more
through porous sandstone to its leaping spill,
escaping in a cascade thrill, down to the Virgin River,
slipping through slot canyons south to coulees and gulches,
creeks and arroyos, to sinkholes and riparian marshes,
to brackish estuaries and the deltas at the ocean's edge.
You might believe the weeping in its mist ascends
to thunderheads at noon, surviving in the clouds' horizon
and still beyond into your human wish.

Now, touch and try to know:
this water, pure, inert, feels neither pain nor suffering,
transfers nothing in its essence lost or sad to grieve.
Rock doesn't keep time as you do, you who have to die.

Reach out and cup the ancient free-fall
just a moment in your open palms,
the good, cold blood of minerals, the ancient serum.

Joy

*TOMS "One Day Without Shoes" campaign
raises awareness about the millions of people
worldwide who don't own a pair of shoes.
As a sign of solidarity, concerned advocates
go an entire day without wearing shoes.*

Hurrying home barefooted on pavement
makes a ridiculous altruism,
nothing like walking sandy village paths
or herding among the hillsides.
A half-mile walk can't teach
you what it means to race volcanic dust
or pad through mire without an end in sight.

"One Day Without Shoes" makes you guilty
for the sixty pairs you own. Guiltier yet
for thinking you could borrow someone else's poverty,
more foolish than a one-day fast,
which never teaches true starvation.

Halfway home each pebble's sharp surprise
reminds that you can only walk the road you're given
and reminds you: walking on water
was a miracle of incarnation
made for naked, human skin to love.

As a child did you ever fear glass shards
or rogue microbial life?
You followed easily behind your grandfather
who plowed behind his mule,
your bare feet filthy from the loam,
toes gripped the way some would imagine
only jungle primate toes can work.
A balancing along the furrowed hummocks,

a dance on clods. That lost pre-amble now recovered
while you try your best to suffer for a cause
and fail.

A native, resurrected carelessness
takes you back in time
to time you walked barefoot
without a worry someone else would think you poor.
Without a care for poverty at all, no money to your name,
a dirty child without a pair of summer shoes,
with all the time in heaven's name to linger
in plush grasses cool enough to draw down evening dew.
An easy balm, a rare, calm sea of cradling green.
Your worst care in the world then
was a piddling stone bruise on your heel.

Humility

You protest the abundant sympathies
for such a little trouble.
Oh, how awful, friends and colleagues say.
Is this really human suffering—
a broken water heater?
Even in the heart of winter
it comes to nothing worse than
hand-washing dishes in cold water,
a week of piled-up dingy laundry.

You find the small tasks charming,
boiling water on the stove each morning,
time to love the blue ease
of the flame, the shining kettle's promise.
In that time before the whistling,
think of your own people
who drew water from the river or the well
for every Saturday's family bath
in a seventeen-gallon galvanized tub.
Think of people even now
who go more often dirty than not,
people who walk miles for water,
then lug their vessels heaving full
the same miles back.

At the bathroom basin,
think of people who must light a fire
in open air and bathe their children with bare hands.
You pour the kettle's boiling water into cold.
Watch steam rise from the clean white cloth,
a luxury across your flesh.
What little effort it takes to bend
and kneel at the edge of the pure white tub.

Pay grateful attention to the walls,
the ceiling, the warmth inside your house.
The last of the warm water
is just enough to rinse your bowed head
and wash you again completely human.

Confession

The scarred man
whose skull the mother bear chewed
and the woman whose arm the alligator mangled
swear they hold nothing against nature
or those animals,
driven to protect their territory
and eat a decent lunch.

When you were a child and hadn't yet learned
responsibility for where you stepped,
honeybees on the clovered yard would stab their venom
into the tenderloin of your arch.
You howled to watch those fiery stingers
pulse their poison into the web between your toes.

Your entire leg would swell, your breathing shorten,
toxins effervescing toward your heart.
The bubbling soda-and-vinegar salve your mother
daubed on the wounds did nothing to save you
from the carnage of blood-red throbbing,
the poisoned flesh, your fragile skin
stretched thin to rupturing.

You didn't care back then
about the little bees who died,
crushed by the giant unseen of your careless foot.
It's only late in life you understand
sacrifice: the bees died trying
to save the blooming world.

What better intercessor than the bee,
back and forth between hard work and honey,
between the flower and the fruit,
the promise and the sting?

You seek and risk true groveling at the hive,
a doorway closed but humming.

Gratitude

for my cousin Dianne

They can preach all they want
that we're a varied human rainbow:
brown, yellow, white, black, red.
No one is glowing iridescent, phosphorescent,
radiating light works like a jellyfish.
No one's blessed with zebra stripes
or a leopard's dapple,
no clown-fish hue or peacock indigo.

What a drab species.
Naked we're all equally dull,
nothing crayon bright about us from ear to toenail.

So we vivify ourselves with tattoos, rings,
with silver studs and polish, shimmer eye shadow,
hair dye, beards and bright hard-hat helmets.
We adorn ourselves with fabrics posh enough
to provoke Saturn's envy.
And still we don't stand out enough to please us,
pierced and fluttery, prancing on flamboyant, stilted shoes.

Live long enough, and you will learn,
what you used to judge anomalous, even ugly,
will mark the ones you love as rare—gap teeth,
a bald head, the furrowed forehead like a bulldog's,
crooked mouth lines, crow's feet, childhood scars,
a million Howdy-Doody freckles,
the hawk nose, looping lobes,
the blurred cockeye that strays.

Your uncle, farmer, fisherman, his whole life
wore mottled skin from fingertip to shoulder,
the missing pigment of vitiligo puzzle-patches.
Who could bear, you wondered as a child,
the spectacle of such marred hands?
But when he died, you missed the albino shapes
that pieced him all together like a Holstein,
like a grand Appaloosa on the pampas,
his shining piebald English setter,
the brown lake trout he loved.

Years later, standing again in the long room
with another family casket, his daughter
stretches out her arms, rolls up her sleeves
as if she's done a magic trick: "Look.
Isn't my skin just like Daddy's?" She is smiling.
"I look down, and every time, I see *him*.
It's the luckiest thing."

She holds your hands in her hands, pale
with paler blooming patches,
like lagoons of pure white floating on her flesh,
clouds that glow in moonlight
and ascending turn to rain.

Mercy

At your kitchen sink a lightning bug
crawls out of place with water-weighted wings
and only one antenna still intact.
Once it's no longer a larva,
this firefly—like all its kind—can live
at best a month of days.
There seems no need for the trouble
it would take to save it.

But coax the fragile body into incandescent light,
onyx sleek and struggling to survive,
writhing away from the blade of your knife,
resisting with its unlit yellow backside.
And then the barest flicker of its signal.

Maybe this is the last hour of its insignificance.
There on your palm, it crawls its search,
tries and fails again to launch itself in flight,
so tiny a being, weightless to your sense.
Yet you feel the hair-like legs, feet small as capillaries
wandering the whorls of your fingertips.

The flesh on the back of your hand lengthens
into alien terrain for this critter to go tickling,
so like the lightning bugs long dead
you caught to witness wink between your fingers,
laced just so to keep and own, without a qualm to kill.

Saved till morning in the jar
was never salvation at all,
the glass gone dead with brittle shaking.
The balance now is briefer than it was,
with more than half your life behind,
with loss and grief enough to break you.

Stand at the threshold of the back porch
in the open doorway,
let go the dying on its last wings.

Grace

Nature never makes a fool of desert animals.
A fair-weather Sunday sunrise in Nevada,
and the birds—larks and warblers,
phoebes, shrikes, and pipits—stay burrowed
in the brief dewy green on either highway side.
They know the distant lake beds are dry.

But you had to be taught
to recognize a mirage, the desiccated salt flats
spread across far miles. You had to learn from books
there's nothing there but dodgy mirrors of blue atmosphere,
a mammoth pooling hot-air of prevarication.

How gullible and glib. You aim the first car of the day
along these miles, flush nestlings and their mothers
frighted right into your motor's roaring.
Until this morning you have never killed
a creature bigger than a spider.

The thunk and frenzied beat beneath the tires
means first blood on your record,
a killing spree of helpless gore,
the brutish, callous smash of hollow bones,
the little beaks and talons crushed on asphalt,
and in the rearview, feathery blusters spewing up.

Yet on you drive, and kill again, trying to believe
intention was a line you never crossed.
Does it matter that you never meant to harm a soul?

You camp at day's end in a listing aspen grove,
around you cryptic bird call in a cryptic wind.
Your first twilight as a murderer, settled by your fire,

you wonder at an empty earthly aerie
not twenty feet from where you bed down.

The answer there at dark: a little doe comes
on careful hooves and looks into your face,
then curls without one hesitation
in her nest, within your watch,
as if you could be trusted.

Empathy

If you look, the lost and found will glitter all their lessons.

In subtropical sun, lift up a cellophane of snake skin
sloughed off near the sand-pile hills of ants.
And shudder—not afraid of venom
or insects feasting on dead skin—
but to think about the itch in molting such a fragile shrug.
Touch the diamond pattern and you
touch the freedom of those born-again new scales.

Flame tree bean pods clatter in the wind
and scatter where they've fallen, two-feet long and hard as bark.
You squat and gather the ones that litter up the yard
like harmless wooden swords,
amazed by tooth- and beak-marks squirrels and birds
have chewed for meager seeds.
They must have flown away with aching, giddy jaws.

The only other person in your view, the next yard over,
is a young girl on a swing. Above the fence
her blond head shows at the apex lift
of every rise she makes to break through gravity.
After school for hours every day, she swings,
silent under the jacaranda tree.

There's something about her not quite right,
her parents and her teachers and the neighbors know,
not seeing through their worry to what's naturally her.

This afternoon, for once, infuse yourself
beyond the logic of adults imagining
the prison of her flesh and mind,
wishing for what we'd wish to be *normal*.
Feel the pulsing shove and plunge

she feels, her hair like light around her face and skin,
the wind she flings herself into, lurching
and falling back into, that same wind touching
her which touches snakes and bugs and calling birds,
the same sunlight on every bougainvillea bloom,
on leaf and limb and vine, each sundered and apart,
yet all together rapt
with every reaching toward immensity.

Salvation

There may not be a soul
there when you die
to help you.

At their last, so many you had meant to save
were lost alone, and you admit you were relieved,
spared from the horror of their last collapse.

Relinquish all your hubris and your hurt,
your guilt; each death's a singular betrayal,
and not a thing to do with how you feel.

Remember this: In her last days,
you slept in the room with your grandmother,
in a small bed near to hers.
Across the dark you talked a while,
the way when you were little
she would talk you into sleeping,
not beautiful like the whippoorwill song
around her house, not like music,
and yet, marvel now how rare
and singular, the solace of her voice
making a grace like another room
inside her room,
and then her breath and yours
and yours and hers.

When you die there may be no one there at all,
just as she died without you.
But maybe you will think of her
and find somehow her wrinkled, cool
hand on your face,
the sweet voice you still recognize
in the breath she gave to you
in the last words you will say.

Soul

You were never meant to keep yourself,
but hoard away you will,
until you're made a worry-stone,
the barest nubbin in the corner of a pocket,
formless and dun as lint.

There's no place secretive enough
away from those you think might seize
and breathe on your watershed onyx.
In private hold it high against the light
and wait for the prism,
but there is only a cryptic, cloudy,
featureless lost cause, of use to no one.

Try and make of it a precious rarity,
a soapstone carving no one ever sees.
Anonymous in narcissistic dark,
its layers crumble in your hands
like brittle shale broken by lake water,
by the roots of gorse.

Share it, though, and then its storehouse tumbles,
a gift whose hard sheen rouses,
however pebbled and marred
by the most turbulent welters you have known,
the peaceable imperfections,
joys and sorrows too.

You will give, and give again,
and learn to give until each gift polishes you,
smooth and riveting in priceless colors.

Let them pocket you and carry you,
and build of you a cairn to show the way,

a dazzling totem only love can settle,
balanced one by one upon the next,
until you're made whole, gathered there,
perfected at the last
by everyone who held you fast
and knew you well
and wept to wonder how in the world
they might ever let you go.

Grief

The body you loved is not a metaphor,
not even the body of the cat, limp without breath
on the kitchen floor, the body you shook and tried to revive,
the body of soft fur you held in its last shiver,
its sweet face unresponsive, with its loveliest green eyes,
staring and not seeing you ever again,
which had looked at you for years with love.

The cat's body is not a metaphor,
though it made you relive every death,
especially your aunt who cried out
to the ones who loved her not to let her die,
who stood by helpless, who could not save her.

And your great aunt coming home
to find her father dead beside the barn,
who decades later found her husband
dead precisely the same, and now she is a body,
and even one of her children is a body,
and even one of her grandchildren is a body.

There is no metaphor for the body
on the floor, in the yard, the body
still arched in its last anguish in the hospital bed,
the body in the cold room in the casket,
the body in the hearse leading the slow cars,
the body you loved burned to ash
bagged in double plastic in a cardboard box,
the body in an urn.

There is no metaphor for the body's ashes scattered,
no metaphor for the body closed under the pecan wood lid,
or the sleek metal lid under satin,
under the rose cascade, under dirt,

no metaphor either for the dirt or the ashes or the empty air,
which replace the body you loved, no metaphor for the love,
which has no other to belong to now, nowhere to live or breathe.

The body is gone, which held and rooted your love,
and so your love can follow only dirt,
can only roost in ash and air,
a solace full of nothing, a vacuum without remedy.

And so you say to the ones who are left,
who understand your foolishness: "I hate love."

Resurrection

A day will come when you recall
the Christmas Eve you were a child and suffered a fever.
Your mother kept you helpless in your own dark house
while a heaven of everyone else you loved on earth
opened presents and ate and laughed under carnival-bright lights.

It was a little death, a show-and-tell of things to come,
when no one stopped their living just for you.

Someone brought to you in your sick bed
a rag doll with embroidered green eyes,
haint-like, a black-haired farmer's daughter,
replica of the spinster aunt who made her
in a rush, an extra, singular gift, a sorry consolation
you can never love, which you begrudge for being lesser.
She mystifies your childhood with her crookedness.

How many deaths does it take?
Years later and beyond the imperfections
you will recognize in that body: Love.
It has to be, the body of the doll an act of love,
though the one who made her is long dead,
unthanked, the age you are now when she sewed,
a sacrifice, a whim, a wish for you to walk again.

She'll teach you from her grave to clobber every sorrow.
No matter no one ever taught you how to sew.
Take up your rolling pin and stand for hours
at the kitchen counter
and cut out homemade sugar cookies
for children who aren't your own,
childless like that old aunt.

Put away the shapes you favor: snowflake, wreath,
and star, the boring bell and candy cane.
Instead take out the wild patterns they will love:
the lion they'll save for last, the gorilla and rhinoceros
they'll wish they could keep forever,
the giraffe whose delicate neck they'll laugh to break,
the tiger's tail and elephant's trunk they'll nibble
and keep nibbling until there's next to nothing left
and only crumbs remain, the spirit of your gift
at the bottom of a brightly colored paper box.

Love

Love bears all things, believes all things,
hopes all things, endures all things.
1 Corinthians 13:7

You think at first the birds
are loblolly pine cones thudding to the porch
after the night-before storm.
But they flutter, two black-capped chickadees,
their chase-in-flight broken by the window
you have only just now washed sky blue.

There is nothing to be done
but kneel down, like this, and bear witness.
Look into the black-eyed blink of suffering,
and coo your comfort at the beaks which cannot speak,
opening and shutting, necks straining at their ruin.

One chickadee on its plump side struggles
crooked, legs curled in anguish, digging
against its racing breast.
Its mate rests upright, blue beautiful claws splayed,
immobilized. You smooth its ebony crown
even as your self sinks, thinking
that its dying will take all day.

Only then the seeming worst-hurt bird leaps up and flies,
a ragged path, and only up
onto the windowsill, but then the second too.
They flicker in tandem onto the wavering hemlock branch
above, then out of your little life.

Isn't it right that you walk away shaken, thinking
their revival could have gone another way?

It could have been you weren't there to see
and never saw at all
or, even seeing, gave up waiting for the answer.

EPILOGUE

The music is not in the notes, but in the silence between.
—Wolfgang Amadeus Mozart

Aionios

As it was in the beginning, is now,
and ever shall be: world without end.
"Glory Be"

in memory of Greg Underwood

Surely you didn't think you could see
all the way across to the other side, did you?

Silvery waves snow-blind you nearly
to eternal tears, squinting into relentless, blathering wind.
Eventually you'll have to shoulder into hurricanes
of sidewise crashing riptide.

Trembling won't do you any good
against the undertow's gravity and the task
of putting one foot ahead of the next,
the sparest bravery you have left, wrecked frail
beside the icy sliding foam that wants
your heels washed way down,
toes sucked into sinking sand.
You'll surely tumble under, wayward, spellbound,
toward what and when and where unknown.
Try at last to accept the certain calamity of horizon,
which always ruins the self as is,
as was.

Is it the sun or moon
here, coming up or setting?
There's barely light enough to see by
beside the water's mirror edge,
illumination emanating from that plunge
of fiery cold, the distant bruise of wilderness.
Is it hours or only minutes that you've faced

away from all you ever knew
and toward an unseen shoreline.

Alone you must step forward, alone
swim or drown with nothing
to your name besides
your name.

Your name.
You hear a voice so faint
you think at first it's just a whisper in your ear.
Someone waving wildly
calls to you far down the strand,
and more in tow out of the spray.
Glad with running now, they run
toward you.
You recognize, without one doubt,
that home has found you safe at last,
and love.

NOTES

The following are brief definitions of the Greek terms, which head the sections, each of which implies an ethos for the poems in its section:

POIESIS suggests the pure creative urge, the natural, cosmic state of creation from which all naive, nascent, and even childlike energy arises.

GNOSIS suggests knowing, in both the positive and the negative sense of becoming aware, alluding to the idea that knowing is powerful but comes with great responsibility.

APHESIS suggests resolution, sought intentionally or granted as by grace, and—though imperfect— even salvation.

EPILOGUE, the "afterword" is from the Greek "epilogos," which means literally what follows words. What exists outside of language?

AIONIOS suggests "aeons," or eternity, the mysterious infinite, which comes after the edge between the last breath and death, but which has also been ever ongoing. The always.

Susan O'Dell Underwood directs the creative writing program at Carson-Newman University in Jefferson City, Tennessee. Besides two chapbooks (*From* and *Love and Other Hungers*) her poems, essays, and stories have appeared in a variety of journals and anthologies, including *Oxford American, North Carolina Literary Review, Southern Humanities Review, Crab Orchard Review,* and *The Southern Poetry Anthology.* She holds an MFA in Creative Writing from the University of North Carolina at Greensboro and a PhD in English from Florida State University. The first chapter of her novel *Genesis Road* won the Tennessee Arts Commission Grant for Literature. She and her husband, artist David Underwood, run Sapling Grove Press, devoted to underserved writers, artists, and photographers in Appalachia. For more information visit: susanodellunderwood.com and saplinggrovepress.com

CPSIA information can be obtained
at www.ICGtesting.com
Printed in the USA
BVHW071920040123
655557BV00003B/105